FROM RESENTMENT TO FORGIVENESS

A Gateway to Happiness

FROM RESENTMENT
TO FORGIVENESS

A Gateway to Happiness

Francisco Ugarte

Scepter

Copyright © 2008 Scepter Publishers, Inc.
(800) 322–8773 / www.scepterpublishers.org
All rights reserved

Fifth printing March 2014

ISBN 978–1–59417–065–2

Text composition in Monotype Times New Roman

Printed in the United States of America

CONTENTS

INTRODUCTION

We all have a natural desire to be happy. But for most people one of the biggest obstacles to attaining happiness is resentment. Even those who seem to have almost everything they need to be happy may be rendered unhappy by a host of resentments that embitter their lives. It's easy to see how widespread this problem is: just look at the critical tone of so many conversations, the anger, the complaints and lamentations, the excuses, negative thoughts, frustrations, the distancing of person from person, family divisions, marriage breakdowns, eagerness for vindication or vengeance, labor disputes, social problems, and even conflicts between nations. We need to face up to this problem, analyze it, and try to find a solution.

Considering how widespread the problem is and how vitally important, it seems surprising that not much has been written about resentment. The subject is seldom discussed in depth. Rarely are the motives behind the many personal and collective conflicts arising from this evil examined. Perhaps this reflects an unconscious reluctance to confront a sad situation in which we all share in some way or another. Lacking a quick fix, we prefer to be silent.

It takes a certain daring to break this resistance and undertake to discuss resentment. Honesty obliges me to point out that other people have had a hand in this present task, and without them I could not have carried it out. I refer particularly to the various groups that have taken part in the classes, conferences, and seminars I have given on this subject. Their contributions were crucial for correcting certain ideas, enriching others, and adding new ones.

The study of resentment demands that we clarify its nature, since the first step in solving any problem is to understand it. It's also necessary to analyze its manifestations and negative effects. But above all we need to offer specific solutions whose eminently positive focus will help to avoid future resentments while eliminating those one already suffers from. Such solutions, as we shall see, are varied and are based on the human and supernatural strengths that everyone has available: focusing one's intellect, strengthening one's will and character, properly channeling one's emotions, interior dispositions, values, and virtues, and finally relying on the help of God.

Above all, the most important means for resolving the problem of resentment is forgiveness, which in itself includes many complexities. Some people take forgiveness as a sign of weakness; others consider it opposed to reason because it goes against justice. Some think forgiveness must be conditioned on the settling of accounts or, still better, on the aggressor's making amends. Still others insist that they forgive but are not ready to forget; or consider it reasonable to forgive only up to a certain point, or consider themselves unable to forgive a particular offense, even though they would like to. We shall address these attitudes more closely in what follows.

Difficult as it is to study forgiveness, it is even more difficult to live out this virtue in practice. Yet it is one of the most important resources available to us for the attainment of happiness. It can resolve, in a fundamental way, the principal obstacle to happiness: resentment.

In my view, human reason cannot explain forgiveness from a purely anthropological perspective. Only by turning to the supernatural order, with the help of theology, can one clarify certain facets of a subject which has an aspect of mystery. In the same way, in the practical order there are situations that can only be forgiven with divine help because forgiving them surpasses human strength.

The discussion of forgiveness that follows here aims to offer arguments that make it easier to practice by pointing to the benefits that derive from it as well as the path to happiness that opens up for someone truly disposed to forgive. I make one suggestion to the reader: to get the most out of what you are about to read, try to be sincere with yourself, especially when it comes to matters that touch on your own situation.

THE POISON OF RESENTMENT

The philosopher Max Scheler calls resentment "a self-poisoning of the mind"[1]—that is to say, a poisoning of our interior that we do to ourselves. How can we avoid this poison or eliminate the resentments we already have? First, we have to understand their nature: what they are, where they come from, how they act within us.

Resentment usually appears as a reaction to a negative stimulus that wounds our "ego." It's usually a response to an offense or aggression. Obviously, not every offense produces resentment; but every resentment is preceded by an offense. Let us begin by analyzing the kinds of injuries we can receive and their characteristics.

The causes of resentment

The offense that causes resentment can be, first of all, someone's *action* against me: a physical attack, insult, or slander. Secondly, it can take the form of an *omission*—when I don't receive something I expect, such as an invitation, a thank-you for service rendered, recognition of an effort I've made. Third, unlike cases of action or omission, offense can be attributed not to a particular person, but to *circumstances*: thus,

[1] Max Scheler, *Ressentiment* (New York: Schocken Books, 1972), p. 45.

someone can resent his poverty, a physical defect, or ill health.

In any of these cases, the stimulus that causes the reaction or resentment can be real, and the subject can judge it with *objectivity*. Or it can have a real foundation yet be *exaggerated* by the subject, as when someone thinks he has received a serious blow even though he has hardly been touched, or feels he is never thanked for his services when on one specific occasion he isn't thanked, or thinks he is suffering from an advanced case of cancer when he only has a tumor in its early stages. Finally, the reaction can be the result of an *imaginary* stimulus, as when someone takes a merely disagreeable phrase as an attempt at defamation, or takes his not being greeted by someone (who may not even have seen him) as a deliberate snub, or considers himself socially excluded through the fault of others. In these instances, resentment depends on how one looks at a particular reality—more specifically, how one judges offenses—with objectivity, in an exaggerated way, or by fantasizing about them. Many resentments, then, are completely gratuitous. They are based on exaggeration or on imagining situations or deeds that no one intended or caused.

The personal response

Resentment is a reaction against aggression. If reason does not intervene to channel or rectify the reaction, it has a negative character. It consists in the response to an offense which one experiences intimately. Thus, the determining element in resentment is not so much the offense as the response to it.

How we respond is up to us because we are free. Stephen Covey says that we are not hurt so much by what others do or even by our own mistakes, as by our response to these things. He points out that "chasing after the poison snake that bites us will only drive the poison through our entire system."[2] It's better to try to get the poison out before it spreads.

In the face of every aggression these alternatives exist: we can either concentrate on the one who has offended us by his attack and thus allow the poison of resentment to rise, or we can eliminate the resentment by an adequate response, not allowing it to remain within us. This explains how the same event —say, the collapse of an enterprise or an identical insult by a powerful person—can be suffered by different people at the same time and with the same intensity, yet in some produce only a transient pain and in others lifelong resentment.

But is it really possible to adjust our reactions to offenses so that they don't turn into resentments? The difficulty arises from the fact that resentment is situated in the emotional part of the personality. Essentially, it is a feeling, a passion, a movement that we experience in a painful way. A person who is resentful *feels himself* to have been wounded or offended

[2] Stephen Covey, *The Seven Habits of Highly Effective People* (New York: Free Press, 1989), p. 91.

by something. Controlling our feelings is not easy. Sometimes we are not conscious of them and they act on us unawares. Thus some people have special difficulty loving others because they didn't receive enough affection from their parents in childhood, but they can't resolve the problem because they don't know its cause. In other cases, resentment is reinforced by reasons that appear to justify it—for instance, when the subject not only feels injured but *considers himself offended*. This intellectual process gives the resentment deeper roots, but it remains a matter of feelings. If a husband is insulted by his wife, he *feels* the insult, and resentment arises in him; if, along with feeling it, he thinks she hates him, this thought will reinforce the hurt he is experiencing.

The intellect as a source of help

These difficulties are not insuperable if we make good use of our reasoning capacity.[3] For example, periodic self-reflection makes it possible to connect the manifestations of our resentments with their causes. We understand what is happening to us, and understanding helps to solve the problem. If in analyzing an injury we have suffered, we try to understand the offender's behavior and any attenuating

[3] "The intellect is formed when one *learns to think*, when one discovers for oneself, when one reads the interior of realities, not when one only hears and circulates what has been said by others. To learn to think is the proper exercise of the intellect." Carlos Llano, *Formación de la inteligencia, la voluntad y el carácter* (Mexico City: Trillas, 1999), p. 12.

circumstances linked to it, our negative reaction will often disappear or at least diminish. A son who grasps that his father is trying to help him by reproving him for his bad behavior may even feel grateful. In this way, by discovering motives or providing reasons, our intellect can help us avoid or eliminate resentments. This is an indirect influence—Aristotle spoke of a political and not despotic rule of reason over the movements of the senses—which modifies our emotional responses and facilitates the disappearance of the poison. This is especially clear when the supposed offense has initially been interpreted in an exaggerated or fantasized manner.

The intervention of the will

Another resource on which we can count is our will. It has the ability to control itself, since as Carlos Llano very pointedly remarks, "The efficient—effective, physical, psychic, real—cause of the will is the will itself."[4] Therefore, when we suffer an attack that hurts us, we can *decide* not to dwell on it and thereby keep it from turning into a resentment. Eleanor Roosevelt used to say, "No one can hurt you without your consent." It is up to us whether or not an offense produces a lasting wound. Gandhi said of attacks and mistreatment at the hands of enemies:

---

[4] Llano, *Formación*, p. 76. On page 108 of this work, the author expresses the same idea in the following words: "The will is moved by itself, in the light of the options that the intellect offers to it or advises."

"They cannot take away our self-respect unless we give it to them." Reacting this way to injuries is not easy, it requires strength of character. Gregorio Marañon says that, "The strong man reacts directly and energetically to attacks and so automatically expels the affront from his mind as though it were some foreign body."[5] Resentful people, on the other hand, lack this "saving elasticity." In this matter strength of will—character—manifests itself in flexibility, not rigidity, since its function is to eject the offense, not permitting it to become a wound that infects the person's whole interior.

It is different with someone who lacks the capacity of directing his response because of weakness of character and will. Besides provoking a negative emotion, the offense is retained, and the feeling persists. Indeed it is experienced again and again as time passes. It is in this that resentment precisely consists: "It is a re-experiencing of the emotion itself: a renewal of the original feeling."[6] The Latin root of resentment is *sentire* (to feel): thus *re-sentire* or resentment.

This is no mere remembrance or intellectual consideration of the offense or the causes that produced it. It is a far cry from recalling an offense without resentment, as can be done when there is no lingering negative feeling. By contrast, resentment is a re-

[5] Gregorio Marañón, *Tiberio: Historia de un resentimiento* (Madrid: Espasa-Calpe, 1981), p. 29.

[6] Scheler, *Ressentiment*, p. 39.

feeling, a return to the feeling of pain that remains within one, like a poison that affects one's interior health. The affront one has received stays buried deep in one's mind, perhaps not even noticed; "there within, it incubates and ferments its bitterness";[7] and this can spread in us, ending up by influencing our actions and reactions.

Some people who feel resentment can describe the offenses they have suffered with such a wealth of detail that one would think these events had just happened. Ask them when these terrible things took place, however, and they may say decades ago. The detailed description of what happened is a sign that the hurts have been brooded upon, and turned over and over in the victim's mind so that the wound has remained open. "Resentment means feeling offended and not forgetting."[8]

Weakness of will also gives rise to resentment for another reason, one more subtle but certainly real. When a person does not get what he wants, or fails to accomplish what he sought to do, the will influences the intellect to distort reality and devalue what could not be attained. In his book *Love and Responsibility*, then-bishop Karol Wojtyla speaks of resentment as arising from a lack of objectivity in judgment and evaluation originating in weakness of will. He points out that in this regard resentment has the distinctive

[7] Marañón, *Tiberio*, p. 26.

[8] Enrique Rojas, *La ilusión de vivir* (Mexico City: Temas de hoy, 1999), p. 140.

characteristics of the cardinal sin of sloth which St. Thomas defines as "a sadness arising from the fact that the good is difficult."[9]

To feel, to lament, or to resent

How one reacts to stimuli can be closely related to temperamental factors. For example, an emotional person feels an affront more than a non-emotional person; a subordinate will retain his reaction to being offended more than a colleague or superior; an active person has more resources to serve as outlets for the blow delivered by an offense than a passive person does. Culture and education, together with genetic makeup, also influence how we react and, therefore, the origin and expression of resentment. Passivity is characteristic of one way of reacting to offenses. The offended party simply withdraws or distances himself from the aggressor—for instance, by refusing to speak to him or her. One writer humorously describes his countrymen as so touchy that they take offense if someone brushes against their clothes or involuntarily nudges them in a crowded bus or greets them with a solemn face because he has a toothache.[10]

Sometimes the reaction to offenses manifests itself in complaints and verbal protests. This is the

[9] Karol Wojtyla, *Love and Responsibility* (New York: Farrar, Straus, Giroux, 1981), p. 143.

[10] See J. A. Peñalosa, *El mexicano y los 7 pecados capitales* (Mexico City: Paulinas, 1985), pp. 69–70.

case, for example, of the older brother in the parable of the prodigal son. When the older son returns home and hears the celebration going on, and learns the reason for it, he complains to his father, "you never gave me a kid that I might celebrate with my friends. But when this son of yours came who has devoured your living with harlots, you killed for him the fatted calf." He obviously feels deeply hurt. His self-esteem is wounded, and his anger "prevents him from accepting this returning scoundrel as his brother. With the words 'this son of yours' he distances himself from his brother as well as from his father." [11]

On the other hand, when one's sense of having been offended includes a desire for vindication, vengeance, or getting even, this is a resentment in the classical meaning of the term. The person not only feels the offense he has suffered, but joins to it a feeling of rancor and hostility toward the persons who caused the hurt. He is moved toward revenge, a balancing of accounts; things may not be left as they are. In effect: "You have hurt me a lot. I will pay you back for that, sooner or later, come what may." [12] Phillip Lersch says: "Vengeance always includes a settlement of accounts. . . . Only in knowing that the other has suffered an equal misfortune, the same damage, will the [resentment] of the one who has

[11] Henri Nouwen, *The Return of the Prodigal Son* (New York: Doubleday Image Books, 1992), pp. 81–82.

[12] Enrique Rojas, *Una teoría de la felicidad* (Madrid: Dossat 2000, 1996), p. 238.

suffered an offense be alleviated." [13] In these cases, therefore, the reaction includes the intention of doing something proportionate to the injury one has received.

Sometimes it happens that for one reason or another the resentful person cannot act against the one he feels has hurt him and his action instead falls on someone who had nothing to do with what happened. The father of a family who is aggressive at home often is channeling resentments acquired in his professional life and turning his frustrations on his wife and children. Similarly a woman hurting inside may externalize her situation, not by aggressive behavior but by irritation and bad humor that indirectly express her pain. This may be profoundly disruptive for her family who depend on her to be conciliatory, calm, and cheerful.

The resentful person retains the offense interiorly because he does not want to forget it. He is pained at his treatment at a particular moment and in certain specific circumstances, which, as was said, he remembers in detail, having repeatedly recalled the event whenever reminded of it. Resentment then can explode years after the event that gave rise to it and lead to taking the long-awaited revenge. Years of waiting and brooding can produce unimaginable actions.

---

[13] Philipp Lersch, *La estructura de la personalidad* [orig. *Der Aufbau der Person*] (Barcelona: Scientia, 1974), p. 141.

A poison to be avoided

Though his intention may be to hurt someone else, the real damage is suffered by the resentful person. It is wisely said that "resentment is a poison that I take, hoping that it will hurt someone else." The person against whom the rancor is directed may not even know about it, while the rancorous person suffers a kind of internal erosion. Poison destroys an organism, and resentment produces frustration, sadness, and bitterness in the soul. It may well be the worst enemy of happiness, as we mentioned earlier, inasmuch as it prevents people from viewing their lives positively and alienates them from the good proper to human beings.

Understanding the nature of resentment is the first step toward avoiding or eliminating it. Summing up what has been said up to this point, we can say that resentment is a negative emotional reaction to a stimulus perceived as an offense against our self-esteem that remains within one and is lived and experienced again and again. The stimulus that provoked the resentment might be an action, omission, or circumstance, seen objectively or in an exaggerated manner, or even simply imagined. When the reaction to the aggression is purely passive it can be called "hurt feelings." Resentment in general, properly speaking, includes the active aspect of seeking vengeance.

There are steps to take that can serve as an antidote to this poison. In many cases, the triggering event may have been evaluated and interpreted erroneously or else a weak will fails to prevent resentments from taking root. When the intellect can reflect[14] and judge events objectively, without exaggeration and imagining, and when it is able to understand the motives and circumstances that led the supposed attackers to act as they did, then many resentments are reduced in intensity or may even disappear. If, moreover, the will is strong and does not consent to the offenses received, it will not allow wounds to remain and fester, but will expel them like foreign bodies. In that case the effects are reduced to painful but passing feelings; lacking the characteristics proper to resentment, they do not have its poisonous effect.[15]

This positive response is much more likely if we count on the help of God, who enlightens our intellect, helping us to be objective and discerning, and gives strength to our will—to our character—so that we don't overreact to offenses.

---

[14] "The formation of the intellect consists above all in the formation and exercise of expressly reflexive knowledge." Llano, *Formación*, p. 36.

[15] There is, among others, an indispensable recourse, in the cases of real offences, which is forgiveness, and an analysis of this will be carried out later in this work.

2

THE RESENTFUL PERSON

Resentment comes easy to some people; they readily *feel*, they react disproportionately to a slight stimulus or naturally hoard unfounded resentments. Sometimes particular actions can produce those effects—a critical comment, a correction, a look of indifference or disdain, a particular tone of voice, an ironic comment. At other times an omission does the trick—as when one feels wounded because he is not congratulated on his birthday, because someone does not greet him, because he isn't thanked or invited to a party; perhaps he feels that people don't appreciate what he does, don't take him into account, don't ask his opinion, don't pay attention to him. When things like these cause a person to feel as if the world were collapsing and he had suffered a grave insult, or to feel sad and full of bitterness, he needs to ask himself if he is reacting normally.

To resent or to be resentful

We usually say a person is feeling resentment when he responds to some happening by experiencing interior hurt—hurt that he retains. When the resentment has become permanent, we say the person is not just feeling resentment, but is resentful. Such a person is continually reacting, sometimes aggressively and even to stimuli with no offensive content. Operative in many such cases is some problematical personal situation—a personal failure or some notable physical defect[1]—that the person has not been able to accept and that weighs him down permanently, consciously or unconsciously.

Feeling resentment and being resentful have many different degrees, but all have certain common features that make one susceptible to resentment. What are these interior dispositions? Can they be resisted, and with what means? The answer to these questions can save us many problems, and point us toward the path leading to true happiness.

Egocentrism and self-forgetfulness

The tendency to focus on oneself, to make oneself the center of one's thoughts and the point of reference of all one's actions, is *egocentrism*. It is the principal ally of resentment. The egocentric person makes himself very vulnerable by attaching too much importance to whatever refers to himself. The negative things about other people tend to produce a disproportionate reaction. Subjectivity then becomes a kind of echo chamber in which offenses reverberate, feeding resentment and producing unhappiness. The psychiatrist Enrique Rojas says that "one of the things that causes most sadness to people is *egolatria* (self-worship), the frequent origin of useless suffering produced by an excessive preoccupa-

[1] See Max Scheler, *Ressentiment* (New York: Schocken Books, 1972), pp. 75–76.

tion with the personal, exaggerating its importance too much."[2]

As St. Josemaría Escrivá said, "People who are constantly concerned with themselves, who act above all for their own satisfaction, . . . cannot avoid being unhappy even in this life. Only if a person forgets himself and gives himself to God and to others . . . can he be happy on this earth, with a happiness that is a preparation for, and a foretaste of, the joy of heaven."[3] If self-forgetfulness is the way to happiness, it is also the best antidote to resentment, since it greatly reduces the echo-effect of offenses and makes it easier to put them out of our minds.

How do we forget ourselves? Through dedication to God and to others, that is, living outside ourselves in a positive way, with the aim of serving others and God: others, because our acts improve them, help them progress in all senses; God, because we set out to fulfill his will.

Sentimentalism

Feelings play a very important role in behavior. They are a source of energy that intensifies human action, and strengthens the decision to fulfill one's duty. As the *Catechism of the Catholic Church* observes, willing, unsupported by feeling—with its source in the

---

[2] Enrique Rojas, *Una teoría de la felicidad* (Madrid: Dossat 2000, 1996), p. 235.

[3] Josemaría Escrivá, *Christ Is Passing By*, 2nd ed. (New York: Scepter, 1974), no. 24.

heart—is not enough: "Moral perfection consists in man's being moved to the good not by his will alone, but also by his sensitive appetite . . . by his *heart*." [4] Feelings in combination with will are a force that can move one to do good. Moreover, when we put our heart into things we ought to do—especially if they concern people—the human quality of our actions is greatly enhanced; whereas absence of feeling produces coldness or indifference. And this is not pleasing to God, to judge by his words to those who are insensitive: "A new heart I will give you, and a new spirit I will put within you; and I will take out of your flesh the heart of stone and give you a heart of flesh." [5]

But to play a positive role in behavior, feelings must be governed by intellect and will. When people do not control their feelings but are dominated by them, the result is *emotionalism*. Sensible stimuli produce exaggerated reactions where rational control of emotions is lacking. Any offense or aggression can generate an exaggerated response that easily turns into resentment. Feelings, if they are not subordinated to the higher powers, tend to be egocentric: they double-back upon the person who is their source. Affection in such a case becomes self-seeking: one loves in order to receive affection, compassion, or some other satisfaction. And as we have seen, egocentrism notably favors the rise of resentments.

[4] *Catechism of the Catholic Church*, nos. 1770, 1775.
[5] Ezek 36: 26.

The solution to emotionalism consists in strengthening the will so it is not dominated by passions and feelings, but instead channels them in the direction indicated by right reason. As muscles acquire and maintain strength by continual exercise, so the will is strengthened by the pursuit of more or less arduous goods: for example, the daily effort to live order in one's work, by beginning and ending on time, working with intensity, and bringing jobs to completion.

The imagination

The imagination also has a strong influence on resentment. Although it can enrich our perceptions, favor creativity, and help us find solutions to problems, it can also get out of control and operate indiscriminately on its own. In that case it separates us from reality, deforms our knowledge, and can be a source of interior complications. An uncontrolled imagination exaggerates things, so that, for example, a small offense is interpreted as a major attack or an apparent omission is seen as an attempt to demean, humiliate, or show hostility. In this way uncontrolled imagination often gives rise to gratuitous resentments that proceed from imaginary offenses.[6]

In these cases, one's capacity for self-criticism

[6] "Most of the conflicts arising in the interior life of many people are products of their own imagination: 'the things people have said, what they are thinking, whether I am appreciated . . .'. The poor soul suffers, through his pathetic foolishness, harboring suspicions that are unfounded." Josemaría Escrivá, *Friends of God* (New York: Scepter, 1981), no. 101.

must come promptly into play in order decisively to cast off imagining before it gets out of hand. This requires a personal struggle that, with God's help, will allow us to direct imagination properly, lest it become an enemy within and make us susceptible to resentment. We learn to control imagination only by continual effort.

A vicious circle

Failure to control one's feelings plus failure to control imagination creates a complicated vicious circle. Feelings or passions act on the imagination, provoking it to see reality in a distorted way, as when someone imagines an opponent is trying to kill him, when that is not his intention at all. At the same time, the imagination affects the feelings, provoking a more intense emotional response: as the attacker's malice is exaggerated, anger swells. The process easily becomes a vicious circle in which bad leads to worse and worse hastens to become worst. If the vicious circle takes shape in an egocentric person who tends to retain grudges, the inevitable result will be a heightened likelihood of taking offense at other trivial or even imaginary provocations. The immaturity of teenagers and their tendency to focus on themselves makes them especially prone to err in this way.

Insecurity

Resentment is a negative emotional reaction that remains within one. Its permanence causes the experience of being wounded—a result of a perceived offense—to recur over and over again. Linked to all this is a weakness—an inability to achieve "closure." This lack of the strength of character needed to dismiss offenses often proceeds from lack of self-confidence. A person with low self-esteem lacks confidence in himself and lives in constant fear of being offended, ignored, or rejected by others. This insecurity expresses itself in various ways that can encourage resentments and ordinarily are linked to egocentrism.

Some people experience a disproportionate need for affection and think of love exclusively in terms of receiving. These people who want to be loved but seem unable to love others show signs of immaturity. When this need to be loved becomes overly important, they become "dependent on the affection they receive. People like this are so subordinate to those who give the affection they need that they end up reducing and even losing the sense of their freedom."[7] Then the innumerable expectations that others fail to satisfy come to be seen as unforgivable omissions.

Insecurity inclines one to seek attention in various ways. People learn at an early age that being sick or injured is a good way of getting attention. Friends and relatives gather around and we enjoy feeling important. Most of us get over this ploy but some

[7] A. Polaino-Lorente, *Una vida robada a la muerte* (Barcelona: Planeta, 1997), p. 200.

people don't. It may be quite unconscious. "However, the fact remains that those people who feel loved and secure have far less illness and 'accidents' than those who don't."[8] When the latter fail in their efforts to be the center of attention, they feel ill and easily develop resentments.

If insecurity is associated with a degree of pessimism, a person may consider himself a victim and feel sorry for himself: they don't like me, they don't appreciate me, they don't pay any attention to me, etcetera. This *victimism*, typically gives rise to complaints that seldom attain what they aim at: "A complainer is hard to live with, and very few people know how to respond to the complaints made by a self-rejecting person. The tragedy is that, often, the complaint, once expressed, leads to that which is most feared: further rejection."[9]

In extreme or pathological cases, insecurity can become an obsessive fear of being offended. And this can lead to a growing pile of resentments that are difficult to control. Basically innocent acts of others are considered a menace to one's ego or an affront. Such "erroneous interpretations can turn into real fantasies of persecution or danger, and can give rise as a result to an aggressive and violent response with ideas of vengeance for an injury not suffered but

[8] Andrew Matthews, *Being Happy!* (New York: Price Stern Sloan, 1990), p. 26.

[9] Henri Nouwen, *The Return of the Prodigal Son* (New York: Doubleday Image Books, 1992), pp. 72–73.

erroneously interpreted as such, or to flight and isolation to avoid those constant 'attacks.' " [10] In general, exhaustion and sickness which weaken a person physically or psychically encourage resentment by lowering the mechanisms of defense that enable one to manage one's reactions to offenses.

Overcoming insecurity

How can one combat insecurity and its various manifestations, in order to reduce the tendency to resentment? Here are a few suggestions.

• Be clear about one's mission in life, so that the meaning of one's life is consistent with one's goals and the means adopted to reach them. Goals and means should of course coincide with God's plan for us.

• Grow continually as a human being, by acquiring virtues and perfecting those already possessed. This will lead to a growth in self-esteem that is consistent with real humility that involves knowing the truth about oneself.

• Strengthen character by pursuing sound goals that require self-conquest.

• Live for others. Concentrate on serving them while forgetting about oneself.

• Evaluate one's personal abilities and qualities— without losing sight of one's defects—in order to find support in them. Also evaluate the good results one

[10] B. Quintanilla, "Venganza y resentimiento," in *Istmo*, no. 226 (Mexico City, 1996), pp. 26–27.

attains in any area. See God as the source of one's capabilities and the results they produce.

• Foster trust in others—the awareness that we can count on them and are supported by them.

• Be aware that we are children of the infinitely good and powerful God.

Gratitude

Especially effective in avoiding resentment, because it is directly opposed to egocentrism and other negative interior dispositions, is gratitude based on recognition of gifts and benefits received. It involves discovering all that is positive in life and receiving it as a gift that moves us to give thanks. Resentment, on the other hand, prevents us from seeing life as a gift. It makes us think people aren't giving us what we deserve.[11]

In contrast, someone who neither expects nor demands anything for himself rejoices at what he receives and ordinarily considers it more than he deserves. Usually, too, he wants to reciprocate, though often he considers himself unable to do so in proportion to what he has received. Says Dr. Polaino-Lorente: "When a person feels loved by many others, without really meriting it, he naturally understands that affection, and his own life, as a gift. Gratitude is inevitable then." And the only way we can really repay those others is by loving in return.[12]

[11] See Nouwen, *The Return*, pp. 72–73.
[12] Polaino-Lorente, *Una vida*, p. 200.

Someone who acts and reacts like this is practically incapable of developing resentments. Gratitude, like any other habit, can be acquired and developed by the repetition of acts: interiorly recognizing gifts received, exteriorly expressing thanks and trying, to the extent of one's ability, to correspond with actions. Thus the tendency to resentment is overcome.

3

TO FORGIVE ... AND ... ?

To excuse and to forgive

If I stumble while walking along the street and, losing my balance, involuntarily knock down a passer-by, I ask pardon. If the victim realizes that my action was truly involuntary, he pardons or excuses me in the awareness that I was not at fault. But if that same passer-by insults his wife when he gets home, it isn't enough for him to ask to be "pardoned" or "excused": he should ask for forgiveness, because he is guilty of the offense.[1] We "excuse" the innocent and "forgive" the guilty. To excuse is an act of justice, because the offender is not really guilty and has a right to be excused; but forgiveness transcends justice, because the guilty person does not "deserve" to be forgiven. To forgive is an act of love and mercy.[2]

It is easier to excuse than forgive. Realizing that someone is not guilty, I have no trouble excusing

[1] "Only if one has done something *on purpose*—in other words, [if one] has done what he wanted to do and acted freely— can he need to be forgiven." André Comte-Sponville, *A Small Treatise on the Great Virtues* (New York: Henry Holt, 2001), p. 123.

[2] To excuse what is excusable "is not Christian charity; it is only fairness. . . . To be a Christian means to forgive the inexcusable, because God has forgiven the inexcusable in you." C. S. Lewis, "On Forgiveness," in *The Weight of Glory*, revised and expanded edition (New York: Macmillan, 1975), p. 125.

him. But when the offender is culpable, one's natural reaction, inspired by a sense of justice, is to demand that he accept the consequences of his action and pay for the damage done. In that case forgiveness implies resisting that first spontaneous reaction and, out of mercy, overcoming the inclination to demand what justice seems to dictate. On the other hand, it makes no sense to forgive what is excusable and should simply be pardoned. Yet that can happen if one fails to distinguish between what is excusable and what is forgivable.

In ordinary life, many acts are interpreted as culpable aggression when in reality they involve no intention to offend, as is the case with involuntary omissions. Reflection, along with putting oneself in the other person's place, enables one to take an objective view of such actions or omissions and see that often it is not necessary to forgive—it is enough to excuse—because the supposed aggressor acted from error, ignorance, or simple distraction. Then the injured party escapes the added burden of having to forgive.

At other times, extenuating circumstances reduce the degree of culpability. Consider the father of a family who comes home tired after a difficult day at work and gets annoyed about the loud music his children are listening to; or the wife who doesn't greet her husband as warmly as he expected because her nerves are on edge after a day of coping with household problems. In some cases, too, more permanent circumstances, properly understood, simplify the problem of forgiveness by shifting offensive behavior to the area of the excusable. Parents who truly understand their children aren't surprised when they act as their temperament or stage of life dictate, and often can excuse their offensive behavior without having to forgive them.

This is not a matter of closing one's eyes to reality, but of distinguishing precisely between the culpable and the excusable. If you have a good excuse, you really don't need forgiveness; but if your action needs forgiveness, then it can't be simply excused.[3] Realism leads to understanding others objectively—not regarding them as if they were distant objects or potential enemies, but looking at them with love to discover all the extenuating circumstances that should be taken into consideration in judging them and reserving forgiveness for what is strictly culpable.

Mercy and forgiveness

In the Old Testament, and other ancient legal codes, the *Law of Talion* prevailed, inspired by strict justice: "an eye for an eye, a tooth for a tooth."[4] Jesus came

---

[3] See Lewis, *Weight*, p. 122.

[4] "We must recall that the Old Testament principle "eye for eye, tooth for tooth" (Ex 21: 24; Lev 24: 20; Deut 19: 21) is in no way the canonization of vindictiveness but quite the contrary, an attempt to replace the principle of revenge by the principle of law." Joseph Ratzinger, *To Look on Christ* (New York: Crossroad, 1991), p. 97.

to perfect the Old Law and introduced a fundamental modification that consisted in linking justice to mercy—indeed, even more, subordinating justice to love, which was revolutionary. After him, offenses were to be forgiven, because forgiveness formed an essential part of love. Jesus wasn't just asking for a little more love or that we go a little beyond what justice demands, he asks that we go to the opposite extreme of forgiving rather than demanding justice for oneself.[5]

The mercy that Jesus practiced and demanded of his followers came as a shock, not only to his times but to all times: "You have heard that it was said: 'You shall love your neighbor and hate your enemy.' But I say to you: Love your enemies, and pray for those who persecute you."[6] "To him who strikes you on the cheek, offer the other also; and from him who takes away your cloak do not withhold your coat as well."[7] These demands of love surpassed mankind's natural capacity, because Jesus invited his followers to a goal which did not have limits. In seeking to realize this ideal they could count on God's help. Only in this way could they attempt to do what he was asking them: "Be merciful, even as your Father is merciful."[8]

[5] See José Luis Martín Descalzo, *Vida y misterio de Jesús de Nazaret* (Salamanca: T. H. Sígueme, 1992), pp. 174–175.

[6] Mt 5:43–44.

[7] Lk 6:29.

[8] Lk 6:36.

What does it mean to forgive?

Unlike resentment, forgiveness is not a feeling, nor does it mean that we stop feeling something. Some people suppose they can't forgive certain injuries because they cannot eliminate their effects: they cannot stop feeling the wound, nor the hatred, nor the eagerness for revenge. This can lead to complications in the sphere of moral conscience, especially if it is recalled that God waits for us to forgive in order to forgive us. The inability to cease feeling resentment on the emotional level can be truly insuperable, at least in the short run. Nevertheless, if it is understood that forgiveness operates on a different level from resentment—that is, on the level of the will—a path opens up that leads to a solution.

An employee who has been unjustly fired, a married person who has experienced the infidelity of his or her spouse, parents whose child has been kidnapped—these people can decide to forgive despite the negative feelings they necessarily experience, because forgiveness is an act of the will, not the emotions. To understand the difference between feeling an emotion and making a decision is already an important step in clarifying the problem. Often in life we should act in a way that goes contrary to the direction in which our feelings are pushing us; and when we actually do this, will has taken precedence over emotion.[9] For example, when we feel discour-

[9] "The will, which can move the intellect in its operations, can also exert despotic control over other powers, especially the

aged by failure in a task, but, instead of abandoning it, try again and successfully complete it; when someone has upset us and we feel the impulse to attack, but instead decide to control ourselves and be patient; when we feel inclined toward laziness, but nevertheless choose to work: all these cases demonstrate the ability of the will to control feelings. So does forgiving even when our feelings are telling us not to.

As an act of the will, forgiveness consists in a decision: to cancel the moral debt that someone else contracted with me in offending me and thereby free him as a debtor. It is not a matter of wiping out the offense, for we don't have that power. Only God can return an offender to the moral state he occupied before committing the offense. Yet when we really forgive, we want the other person to be completely freed from the bad action that he committed. Therefore, "to forgive implies asking God to pardon,

---

motor functions: it is able to order the movement of the arms and the legs, direct the direction of one's gaze, of the movement of the tongue, of the operations of the hands. . . . But, on the other hand, it is not possible to exert this kind of control over the appetites, feelings, or movements of the senses, which enjoy a certain autonomy. The will, with the help of the intellect, has to exercise a political type of government, persuading or convincing the sensitive tendencies of the human being, and it has to limit itself to this: when it cannot orient them toward the good, it has to transcend them, step over them." Carlos Llano, *Formación de la inteligencia, la voluntad y el carácter* (Mexico City: Trillas, 1999), p. 142.

because only thus is the offense annihilated." [10] This is a radical way of proceeding, with consequences for the one who forgives. Let's look at them.

Modifying negative feelings

The decision to cancel the offender's debt is an act of love requiring that I wish to eliminate the subjective effects produced in me by the offense—hatred, resentment, the desire for revenge, and so on. When we forgive we "turn off," so to speak, the feelings in us that were caused by the offense. These might have included even hatred, but at least rancor or resentment and the desire for punishment or revenge. We don't "expunge" the wrong we suffered but we no longer feel a grudge against the person who harmed us.[11] As we have said, this decision does not automatically eliminate the feelings generated by the aggression, but it leads to their acceptance, coupled with efforts gradually to modify them.

Negative feelings provoked by the offense can be modified in an indirect way. Instead of trying to repress them directly—which would not work—it is more effective to try to adjust them in a way that changes their meaning. Upon feeling hurt, one can think of the harm the other person has done himself by offending us and feel sorry for him; one can also ask God to help him amend his improper action, even

---

[10] Leonardo Polo, *Quién es el hombre* (Madrid: Rialp, 1998), p. 140.

[11] See Comte-Sponville, *A Small Treatise*, p. 119.

though we are still feeling its effects. Speaking more properly, "it is not in our power not to feel or to forget an offense; but the heart that offers itself to the Holy Spirit turns injury into compassion and purifies the memory in transforming the hurt into intercession." [12]

The cancellation of debt that forgiveness effects deeply involves the person who forgives. One's inner self is no mere spectator, as if of an emotionless business deal. To forgive requires reestablishing the relationship one had with the other before he committed the offense. If it was close, love reappears. Cancellation of the debt while remaining aloof is not enough. No feeling provoked by the offense may cast its shadow on the loving relationship. [13] Someone offended by a friend cannot tell him: "I forgive you, but from now on let's keep our distance." If the forgiveness is genuine, distances must disappear. The one offended must treat the other as if nothing had happened, accept him in spite of the hurt, even though the wound still exists. And since friendship demands reciprocity the other must rectify. There is no rebuilding the relationship, no matter how much the one offended forgives, as long as the offender retains his disposition to give offense.

[12] *Catechism of the Catholic Church*, no. 2843.

[13] "Anyone who knows the meaning of God's love will understand forgiveness in a very different way, for he will not be satisfied that God has canceled his debt . . . He needs God to love him, to continue loving him as he did before, without reserve. . . . All the rest is secondary." José María Cabodevilla, *El padre del hijo pródigo* (Madrid: B.A.C., 1999), p. 139.

Forgiveness and prudence

When someone who has caused an injury intends to go on causing it, a person has every right to join his forgiveness with the prudential steps needed to prevent the other from carrying out his intention. If a visitor robs me or tries to harm someone in the family, I am entitled, along with forgiving, to prevent him from entering the house again. In this way I am not only exercising my right to protect my own, but also showing a desire to help the offender. If forgiving is an act of love, and love consists in seeking the good of the other, I am doing my enemy good by helping him avoid actions that damage him. Along with closing the doors of my house to him, I should do what I can to influence his conduct for the good.

In the same way, the good of the aggressor sometimes can require punitive action on the part of the one who has to forgive. A reprimand, even a punishment, can be compatible with forgiveness if in this one is really seeking the other's good. A mother can energetically scold her disobedient daughter while at the same time forgiving her. She can also impose some punishment if this is the best way to bring about needed change. Often it is necessary to overcome one's feelings if one really seeks the good of the other. It is easier to forgive but remain passive in the face of the other's error, than to forgive and take corrective measures so that he reforms. To forgive does not necessarily mean canceling the punishment or the material debt—in some cases, that would not be good for the offender—but eliminating the moral debt that the other contracted in offending me.

Even after one has forgiven an offense and renounced vengeance, a sense of justice may cause one still to harbor the desire that some third party—fate or God himself—exact vengeance. It's like saying, "I forgive you, but wait until you see what God will do." This is not really forgiving. "Human forgiveness is not the same as making use of divine vengeance as a means to human vengeance. To decide not to take vengeance because God will do it for me is a pretext that goes directly against piety and honor. Therefore, one who knows that in the future God will decide the punishment has to ask: 'forgive all of us.'" [14]

To sum up: forgiving is a radical act of the will that includes objective and subjective elements. On the one hand, there is a decision to cancel the moral debt incurred by the offense, renew one's relationship with the offender, and seek his good. On the other hand, there is an attempt to eliminate the adverse feelings caused by the offense, to substitute or change them into others of a positive nature.

To forgive and forget
While forgiving arises from a decision of the will, forgetting takes place in the sphere of memory, which is not immediately responsive to the will's commands. Deciding to forget an offense and erase it

[14] Polo, *Quién es el hombre*, pp. 139–140.

from my memory is unlikely to succeed. The offense remains in memory's archive despite the will's command to forget. Evidently, then, forgetting is not forgiving. Forgiving and the memory of the offense can coexist.

Still, "I forgive, but I don't forget" usually signifies not wanting to forget, and this "not wanting" is equivalent to not wanting to forgive. When one truly forgives, after all, one cancels the offender's debt, but this is incompatible with the intention of retaining it, not wanting to forget it. Although forgiveness is not forgetting, *to forgive is to want to forget.*

Ordinarily, if the decision to forgive—which includes the desire to forget and not file away insults— has been firm and is maintained, the memory of the offense will begin to fade and will in many cases disappear with the passage of time. But even if this does not happen, forgiveness has been granted, since its essence is not forgetting but deciding to release the offender from the debt contracted. Even though it has not been possible to forget, an eloquent sign that he has been forgiven is that involuntary remembrance of the offense does not affect how one behaves toward the forgiven person. "Perhaps it is not possible to forget, but one has to act as though we had forgotten. True forgiveness requires that we act in this way, because true love 'is not resentful' (1 Cor 13: 5)." [15]

---

[15] Cabodevilla, *El padre*, p. 219.

Can we say, however, that to forget is to forgive? The two acts are not the same, and an offense can be forgotten without having been forgiven—although, if the injury was a major one, forgetting is difficult. Thus, when the offense has been great, forgetting it can be a clear sign that we have truly forgiven it. Jorge Luis Borges, a major Argentinean writer, poignantly describes Cain and Abel meeting, some time after one brother has killed the other. They recognized and greeted each other, then made a fire, sat down and started to eat. Suddenly in the firelight, Cain recognized the mark of the stone on Abel's forehead. He dropped the food he was eating, and asked to be forgiven. " 'I no longer remember—did you kill me or was it I who killed you?', Abel answered. 'Now I know you've forgiven me,' said Cain, "because to forget is to have forgiven. I'll try to forget, too.' " [16]

[16] Jorge Luis Borges, "Leyenda," *Elogio de la sombra*, in *Obras completas*, vol. 2 (Buenos Aires: Emecé, 1996), p. 391.

4

THE MYSTERY OF FORGIVENESS

Why forgive?

The question has its logic: If it's so difficult to forgive, or at least to forgive certain offenses, why do it? Is it worthwhile? What benefits does it bring?

The first reason for forgiving is, as mentioned earlier, that in forgiving, we free ourselves from enslavement to hate and resentment and can recover the happiness that those feelings block. Holding a resentment gives the person we resent a certain power over us. By forgiving the person, we take back the responsibility for our own happiness. In doing this we "release that person from the real or imagined debt owed me, and . . . release myself from the high price of continued resentment.[1]

Forgiveness also makes a lot of sense in regard to our relations with others, including people we are close to and love, yet differ with. Sometimes such differences can lead to insults, which hurt more when they come from those closest to us: parents, children, one's spouse, or friends. If we are ready and able to forgive, those painful situations are overcome and love or friendship is recovered. If we don't forgive, love cools and can even turn into

[1] John S. Powell, *Happiness Is an Inside Job* (Allen, Tex.: Thomas More, 1989), pp. 45–46.

hatred, while friendship, with all its value, can be lost forever.

Aside from these human motives for forgiving, there are supernatural reasons derived from our relationship with God. These in no way contradict the human motives but instead reinforce and complete them. In some extreme situations human arguments lack power to move us to forgiveness. We need higher reasons then. Let's consider what these are.

God made us free and therefore capable of loving him or of offending him through sin. If we choose to offend him and then repent, he can forgive us, but he has established a condition for doing this: first, we must forgive our neighbor who has offended us. We repeat in the prayer Jesus taught us: "Forgive us our trespasses as we forgive those who trespass against us."

But why does God condition his forgiveness on our forgiving and, even more, demand that we forgive enemies unconditionally, that is, even those who do not want to rectify? Obviously, God is not trying to make things hard for us and always wants what is best for us. He deeply wants to forgive us, but his forgiveness cannot penetrate us unless we change our dispositions. "In refusing to forgive our brothers and sisters, our hearts are closed and their hardness makes them impervious to the Father's merciful love."[2] God respects our freedom. He conditions his

<hr />

[2] *Catechism of the Catholic Church*, no. 2840.

intervention on our openness to receive his help. And the key that opens our hearts is the act of freely forgiving those who have offended us, and doing that not just sometimes, but repeatedly.[3]

Not only when he taught us the Our Father, but repeatedly, Jesus insisted on the need for forgiveness. When Peter asked him whether it was necessary to pardon as often as seven times, he answered, "I do not say to you seven times, but seventy times seven."[4] That is to say: forgiveness has no limits. Moreover, he asked that we forgive everyone, including enemies[5] and those who return evil for good.[6] For the Christian, these teachings, dictated by the Master, constitute a powerful reason for forgiveness.

Jesus, the model for all who have faith in him, not only preached forgiveness, but practiced it innumerable times. His life offers many examples of his readiness to forgive, which was perhaps the greatest expression of his love. "Among the various manifestations of charity towards one's neighbor, I would like to consider one which is a most faithful reflec-

[3] C. S. Lewis suggests that it may be easier to forgive "a single great injury" than to forgive "the incessant provocations of daily life . . . the bossy mother-in-law, the bullying husband, the nagging wife, the selfish daughter, the deceitful son." The latter forgiveness is possible, he wrote, only "by meaning our words" when we say, *Forgive us our trespasses as we forgive those who trespass against us.* "There is no hint of exceptions," he points out, "and God means what he says." Lewis, *Weight of Glory*, p. 125.

[4] See Mt 18: 21–22.

[5] See Mt 5: 44.

[6] See Mt 5: 39.

tion of the sentiments of our Redeemer: the promptness with which he forgave."[7] When the scribes and pharisees accused a woman who had been taken in adultery, Jesus forgave her and counseled her not to sin again.[8] When they brought a paralytic on a stretcher for him to cure, he first forgave his sins.[9] When Peter denied him three times, despite being warned, Jesus looked at him, elicited his sorrow,[10] and not only forgave him but restored his position of trust at the head of the Church. And at the culminating moment of Jesus' forgiveness—on the Cross—he prayed for his executioners: "Father, forgive them, for they know not what they do."[11]

When we consider that sin is an offense against God which takes on infinite dimensions for that reason, and that God nevertheless forgives our sins when we do our part, the huge disproportion between divine forgiveness and human forgiveness stands out in bold relief. St. Josemaría's advice takes on fresh meaning: "Force yourself, if necessary, always to forgive those who offend you, from the very first moment. For the greatest injury or offense that you can suffer from them is as nothing compared with what God has pardoned you."[12] —or how often, one

[7] Bishop Javier Echevarría, Pastoral Letter, April 1, 1999.

[8] See Jn 8: 3–11.

[9] See Mk 2: 5.

[10] See Lk 22: 56–60.

[11] See Lk 23: 34.

[12] Josemaría Escrivá, *The Way* (New York: Scepter, 1985), no. 452.

might add. These considerations are always relevant, no matter how badly and how often we've been injured.[13]

Forgive up to what point?

Some offenses seem unforgivable because of their magnitude, because they are against innocent persons, or because of their consequences. Humanly speaking, we can't find sufficient justification for forgiving them. And indeed, as we've seen, forgiveness can't be understood in exclusively human terms in all its dimensions and in all cases. Only from a theological perspective can we grasp that even what seems unforgivable can be forgiven, because "there is no limit or measure to this essentially divine forgiveness."[14] That forgiveness in its essence belongs to God also means that man, to forgive radically, must link himself with God. Only thus, for example, can we explain the touching witness of John Paul II, who, upon leaving the hospital after the assassination attempt of May 13, 1981, visited his attacker, Ali Agca, embraced him, and afterward commented: "I spoke to him as one speaks to a brother who enjoys my trust, and whom I have forgiven."

The all-embracing outreach of forgiveness extends

[13] "The mote and the beam, that is to say, the offenses that I have received from my neighbor and the offenses that I have committed against God. The disproportion between one and the other is incommensurable." José María Cabodevilla, *El padre del hijo pródigo* (Madrid: B.A.C., 1999), pp. 224–225.

[14] *Catechism of the Catholic Church*, no. 2845

also to those offenses that are hardest to forgive: those suffered by the people we love most. In these cases our emotions tell us that to forgive the guilty party is to betray our affection for the victim. But we must not let ourselves be led by emotion. We must try to distinguish between our affection for the beloved person and our forgiveness of the aggressor, which rests upon different, compelling grounds. As much as possible we will try to make love concrete by seeking the good of both parties: the one who has suffered the offense, whom we love naturally, through the help and affection that are due him or her; and the one who has inflicted injury through corrective action that will encourage him to repent and reform.

How to forgive

A person ruled by his imagination, who invents offenses or exaggerates those he receives, as well as someone who can't distinguish between the excusable and the culpable in an "aggressor's" behavior, sees a need of forgiveness where it isn't required. But it is no less a mistake not to see the value of forgiving real offenses and attempting to ignore or forget them instead. Then the effect of the offense remains unresolved because the offense has not been forgiven. Rigorous, objective, accurate analysis is essential. In order to forgive one must be a realist. "We have to have the guts to look hard at the wrongness, the horridness, the sheer wickedness of what somebody did . . . eye the evil face to face and . . . call it what it is. Only realists can be forgivers."[15] Said in another way, "real forgiveness means looking steadily at the sin, . . . in all its horror, dirt, meanness, and malice, and nevertheless being wholly reconciled to the man who has done it."[16] That is the kind of forgiveness we have to ask God to help us show.

In the parable of the prodigal son, the older son cannot forgive his brother for one simple reason: he does not consider that he himself needs forgiveness. He has always behaved well, remained in his father's house, and had no cause to repent. Mother Teresa says: "When we realize that we are all sinners needing forgiveness, it will be easy for us to forgive others. We have to be forgiven in order to be able to forgive. If I do not understand this, it will be very hard for me to say 'I forgive you' to anyone who comes to me."[17] St. John Chrysostom remarks that "one who considers his own sins will be quicker to forgive his companion."[18] Recognizing one's own offenses is nothing other than being humble, and humility is the basis for any good act, especially when the action needs to be moved by love, which is the case with forgiveness. Pride only loves itself, it doesn't consider itself in need of forgiveness and, consequently, can't forgive.

[15] Lewis B. Smedes, *Forgive and Forget* (San Francisco: Harper & Row, 1984), p. 141.

[16] Lewis, *Weight of Glory*, pp. 123–124.

[17] Mother Teresa of Calcutta, *No Greater Love* (Novato, Calif.: New World Library, 1997), p. 110.

[18] St. John Chrysostom, *In Matthaeum homiliae*, 61, 5.

Forgiving also requires courage. That is true of the decision to free the other from his moral debt contracted by the offense, to be steadfast, and to stick to this decision henceforth. Deciding to forgive does not cauterize the wound or banish it from memory. Unless one renews the decision whenever the offense comes to mind, there is a danger of again consenting to the resentment and withdrawing one's forgiveness.

Yet, as we have said, there are times when forgiving is beyond one's ability. Then we must remember that forgiveness in its deepest essence is divine and must ask God's grace to be able to grant it: "The acceptance of God's forgiveness leads to the commitment to forgive our brothers and sisters."[19] St. Josemaría used to say: "You have to forgive! But really, without resentment. Forgiveness is something divine. We men would not know this, if Jesus had not taught it to us."[20]

The effects of forgiveness

To forgive produces great benefits in relations with others and with God. There is mutual benefit for oneself and one's neighbor, while on the supernatural level the heart that forgives becomes capable of receiving divine forgiveness.

Various means of overcoming resentment have

[19] Pope John Paul II, Homily on the Jubilee "Day of Pardon," March 12, 2000, no. 4.

[20] See ibid.; and also Javier Echevarría, Pastoral Letter, April 1, 1999.

been mentioned earlier, but the most profound remedy is forgiveness. Where interiorly I have held on to a wound and it has generated hatred or rancor, the only real solution is forgiving—blotting out the other's debt to me and eliminating, even if only slowly, the poison in my spirit. As resentment disappears, one recovers peace and happiness. Pope John Paul II, his eyes focused on the third millennium, said, "May the joy of forgiveness be stronger and greater than any resentment."[21] Moreover, eliminating resentment also frees one from attachments that produce dependence and slavery and darken one's life. Forgiveness therefore is a path to interior freedom that enables us to look at life positively and orient it toward high ideals.

As the highest manifestation of love, forgiveness brings about the greatest change in the human heart. Whenever we forgive, we experience interior conversion, a true metamorphosis. St. John Chrysostom goes so far as to say that "nothing makes us so like to God as a readiness to forgive."[22]

Someone dominated by resentment looks at others unfavorably, through prejudices arising from hatred and rancor. Upon forgiving, he sees clearly, prejudices disappear, and he can view others as they really are; he may discover and value their qualities that up until then were hidden.

[21] Message *Incarnationis Mysterium* (November 29, 1998), no. 11 (www.vatican.va).

[22] Chrysostom, *In Matthaeum homiliae*, 19, 7.

If resentment is the principal enemy to good relations with others, forgiveness allows one to recover the treasure of friendship and love that seemed lost. How sad it is to lose a friend due to one's inability to forgive. How often does love between two people fade away because each of them is piling up grudges and keeping track of offenses, instead of setting them aside and forgiving them?

When we forgive those who offend us, we allow ourselves to be forgiven by God. And forgiveness is his most explicit manifestation of love for us. God's love in turn is the source of our love for him. To the degree that we know and feel ourselves loved by God, we are led to love him, we desire to correspond to him. Thus we respond to the call to sanctity that he directs to all mankind.

Conclusions

The paragraphs that follow summarize the main solutions presented here to the problem of resentment and the challenge of forgiveness. In effect they sketch a program of personal development aimed at eliminating resentment and exercising forgiveness to attain a higher level of happiness.

• The first thing needed to confront and solve the problem of resentment is to understand its nature as a negative emotional reaction to a stimulus perceived as an offense that remains within the subject with a pernicious effect.

• It's easier to manage resentment if one's judgment

regarding the offense received is objective and neither exaggerated nor imaginary. That requires seeing the true nature of the offense and controlling one's imagination.

• Many resentments vanish when the judgment about the supposed aggression is not only objective but discerning, in that extenuating circumstances are fully taken into account.

• Strength of will helps one dominate feelings and prevent wounds from becoming permanent and turning into resentments. This strength is visible in the firmness and constancy of one's decisions regarding the directing of emotions.

• Self-forgetfulness in service and dedication to others is the best antidote to the poison of resentment.

• The chances of becoming resentment's victim are reduced in one who conquers insecurity through self-esteem, humility, and a personal relationship with God.

• Gratitude, which lies in perceiving the goods we receive and recognizing them as gifts, is the antithesis of resentment. A person who lives the virtue of gratitude will not suffer from resentments.

• When offenses are both real and intended, one can keep them from generating resentments only by forgiving them.

• Since forgiving is an act of mercy, the key to forgiveness is love. Only a person who truly loves is capable of forgiving.

• Forgiveness is an act of the will. Thus the decision to forgive is possible even when our feelings oppose it. Even after forgiveness, of course, one must try to eliminate the negative feelings that remain—for example, by using a wound as an occasion to feel compassion for the one who inflicted it and turning an offense into an incentive to pray for the offender.

• Having pardoned an offender, one should act toward him according to what is best for him.

• Once one has forgiven something, one should try to forget the offense, proceeding as if it were already forgotten and taking steps to re-establish one's former relationship with the offender.

• By knowing Jesus, we can enter deeply into his teachings on forgiveness and try to imitate his example of forgiving without limit.

• Someone who recognizes his own need for forgiveness because of the offenses he has committed is then capable of forgiving others.

• The fundamental reason for always forgiving my neighbor is that God has forgiven me—and offending God through sin is infinitely more serious than any offense I can suffer.

• Even though some offenses lie beyond the human capacity to forgive, what is humanly unforgivable can be forgiven with the help of God.

* * *

BIBLIOGRAPHY

Borges, Jorge Luis. *Obras Completas*. Buenos Aires: Emecé, 1996.

Cabodevilla, José María. *El padre del hijo pródigo*. Madrid: B.A.C., 1999.

Catechism of the Catholic Church. Libreria Editrice Vaticana, 1994.

Comte-Sponville, André. *A Small Treatise on the Great Virtues*. New York: Henry Holt and Co., 2001.

Covey, Stephen. *The Seven Habits of Highly Effective People*. New York: Free Press, 1989.

Echevarría, (Bishop) Javier. Pastoral Letter, April 1, 1999 (www.opusdei.org).

Escrivá, Josemaría. *Christ Is Passing By*, 2nd ed. New York: Scepter, 1982.

———. *Friends of God*. New York: Scepter, 1981.

———. *The Way*. New York: Scepter, 1985.

John Chrysostom (St.). *In Matthaeum homiliae*. In J. P. Migne, ed., *Patres Graeci*.

John Paul II. Homily at the Mass of the "Jubilee Day of Forgiveness," March 12, 2000, no. 4 (www.vatican.va).

———. *Incarnationis Mysterium*. November 29, 1998, no. 11 (www.vatican.va).

Lersch, Philipp. *La estructura de la personalidad* [orig. *Der Aufbau der Person*]. Barcelona: Scientia, 1974.

Lewis, C. S. *The Weight of Glory and Other Addresses*. New York: Simon & Schuster, 1980.

Llano, Carlos. *Formación de la inteligencia, la voluntad y el carácter*. Mexico City: Trillas, 1999.

Marañón, Gregorio. *Tiberio: Historia de un resentimiento*. Madrid: Espasa-Calpe, 1981.

Martín Descalzo, José Luis. *Vida y misterio de Jesús de Nazaret*. Salamanca: T. H. Sígueme, 1992.

Matthews, Andrew. *Being Happy!* New York: Price Stern Sloan, 1990.

Mother Teresa of Calcutta. *No Greater Love*. Novato, Calif.: New World Library, 1997.

Nouwen, Henri. *The Return of the Prodigal Son*. New York: Doubleday Image Books, 1992.

Peñalosa, J. A. *El mexicano y los 7 pecados capitales*. Mexico City: Paulinas, 1985.

Polaino-Lorente, Aquilino. *Una vida robada a la muerte*. Barcelona: Planeta, 1997.

Polo, Leonardo. *Quién es el hombre*. Madrid: Rialp, 1998.

Powell, John S. *Happiness Is an Inside Job*. Allen, Tex.: Thomas More, 1989.

Quintanilla, B. "Venganza y resentimiento." In *Istmo*, no. 226 (Mexico City, 1996).

Ratzinger, Joseph. *To Look on Christ*. New York: Crossroad, 1991.

Rojas, Enrique. *La ilusión de vivir*. Mexico City: Temas de hoy, 1999.

———. *Una teoría de la felicidad*. Madrid: Dossat, 2000, 1996.

Scheler, Max. *Ressentiment*. New York: Schocken Books, 1972.

Smedes, Lewis B. *Forgive and Forget*. San Francisco: Harper & Row, 1984.

Wojtyla, Karol. *Love and Responsibility*. New York: Farrar, Straus, Giroux, 1981.